The Pocketbook of Wisdom

By

Grandmother Kiri Dewes

Australia's Counsel of 13 Grandmothers

Additional copies can be obtained from the publisher:

Vortex Publishing

215 Dalmayne Road

PO BOX 187

St Marys TAS 7215
Australia

+61 418.515.419

First edition Copyright @2020
Kiri Dewes

All rights reserved. No part of this book may be reproduced or utilised in any form or by any means, electronic or mechanical, including photocopying, recording, or any information storage retrieval system, without permission in writing from the publisher.

Printed in Australia

Vortex Publishing Tasmania Australia 2020

Dedicated

to all the indigenous wise
women on this planet

Introductions

The wit and wisdom of Kiri Dewes is known far and wide!

This book is to share her wisdom and experience, profound, moving, funny and just what you need for your daily encouragement.

Grandmother Sue

Sue Christiansen Australia's Counsel of 13 Grandmothers

To sit with Nan and hear her tell her stories and life's lessons truly is an honour.

Kiri Dewes is a proud Maori Women, her journey is inspiring. Nan is the proud Custodian of such ancient wisdom and sacred knowledge.

Her words will awaken a sacred connection within you.

Blessings,

Grandmother Jenny
Jenny Buffa
Australia's Counsel of 13 Grandmothers

"Mai te kōpae ki te urupā, ako tonu ai tātou." "From the cradle to the grave, we are forever learning.

Enjoy this day".

"Never let a fool kiss you and never let a kiss fool you".

"Prayer in the old Maori tradition is as ever present as breathing.

In fact, breathing is a form of prayer and 'peace is not a concept, it is the way the Creator expects us to live".

"When we get too busy to stop and be thankful, we probably need to examine our priorities".

"Today I wish you a day of ordinary miracles. A fresh cup of tea, coffee or whatever, an unexpected phone call or visit, fast lane at the supermarket".

"Slow down and notice the ordinary miracles that occur in your life".

"It's not what we gather, but what we scatter that tell what kind of life we are living. We will not be remembered by our words but by our deeds".

"Being a good person doesn't mean you have to put up with other people's crap.

Move on, life's too short".

"Each day, let us hold love in our hearts for each other and not be drawn into negative things that hinder our journey on this planet".

"Love brings us all together and love also keeps us together. Very thankful, blessed and appreciative to be living in this beautiful Land of the Dreamtime".

"The creator planted a seed of faith in our hearts, so all we had to do was water it with prayers, feed and nurture it with words of the Creator and cultivate it with lots of love".

"The power of compassion is far greater than anything money can do".

"Behind every successful woman should be a tribe of women who have her back".

"Moving on doesn't mean we don't hurt. It's about asking yourself, "How did I screw up, so it doesn't happen again." Something to think about".

"Everything in life is temporary, so if things are going good, enjoy it, because it won't last forever ,and if things are going bad, don't worry, because it can't last forever too".

"Let us be grateful for people who make us happy, for they are the charming gardeners that make our souls blossom".

"No person is ever truly alone. Those who live no more, whom we love, echo still within our words, our hearts and our thoughts." Even time cannot erase them from our thoughts and our hearts".

"If there's someone in your life that you need to forgive, fix it and move on, for life is too short. Feel the weight lift off your shoulders".

"Sometimes we create our own heartbreak because of our expectations".

"Never allow people to make you feel as if you're not good enough. You are the best, so always be proud of who you are."

"Don't start your new day with the thoughts of yesterday, because every day has its own story and your part to play in it".

"The most beautiful form of communication that allows the other person to know beyond a doubt that they matter is a HUG".

"A choppy sea can be navigated." "He moana pukepuke kā ekengia e te waka." If we all contribute, all will be well.

"Don't spend your precious time immersed in rumours, things from the past, negative thoughts or things beyond your control, for it is better to invest your energy in the positive present".

"Always focus our conscious minds on things we yearn for, not things that we fear, for that is the key to success".

"Words are powerful. Your mouth can spit venom or it can mend a broken soul. Words can change your life, inspire a nation and make this world a beautiful place".

"Laughing is good for you, so laugh often long and hard. Laugh till you gasp for breath".

"Taking less than you need is pride, giving more than you can is generosity".

"Love has no culture, race, religion or boundaries. It is pure and beautiful like early morning sunrise falling on a lake".

"Be knowledgeable in pursuit of your dreams, so your efforts and achievements maybe the springboard for future generations to thrive and prosper".

"Make peace with your past, so it won't screw up your present.

"Carrying the spirit of the child into old age means never losing your enthusiasm. This is the secret of genius."

"Dreams are the seedlings of realities"

"What other people think of you is none of your business., so just keep on being you, being real. Just keep on keeping on".

"Making time for the Creator in our daily lives is not a luxury, it is a necessity".

"Life is too short to waste time hating anyone. Fix it, forgive, forget and move on for the sake of your own sanity. It's not worth it".

"Don't compare your life to others. You have no idea what their story is all about".

"Imagination is everything. It is the preview of life's coming attractions."

"Be like a flower, because it never competes with the flower next to it. It just blooms".

"Be someone's sunshine when their skies are grey".

"We each carry deep within us a power far greater than any challenge the world presents us with, because the inner power and authority invested in us by the Creator guides and protects us always".

"Eliminate clutter in your home, the car and your work, whatever it is and allow a new energy to enter your life." It's an amazing feeling.

"Life does not come tied with a bow, but it's still a gift, so make the most of it".

"If ever you're in doubt, remember whose daughter you are and straighten your crown".

"Allow your hopes and aspirations shape your future, not your hurts and disappointments".

"No matter what you are going through, there's always light at the end of the tunnel, and it seems so hard to get to it, but you can do it".

"Having a purposeful life means that your existence impacts others in a meaningful way".

Enjoy this day.

"Life is a school and we are here to learn. Problems are lessons that come and go. What we learn from will serve us for the rest of our lives".

"Never underestimate your value. You are unique, there will never be another you. You are special. Don't ever forget that. Head high, walk tall and greet each day with a smile".

"Two things define you- your patience when you have nothing- your attitude when you have everything".

"You are never too old to dream another dream".

"A mirror reflects your image, but your soul reflects your beauty".

"There is no wifi in the forest but be assured you will find a better connection".

"The people you are closest to, seem to be the ones that hurt you the most. That is why heartbreak is so hard to deal with, why death is so painful".

"Earth and sky, forests and fields, lakes and rivers, seas and mountains are excellent teachers. What we learn from them, we can never learn from books".

"The devil is never too busy to rock the cradle of a sleeping backslider".

"One of the basic differences between humans and the Creator is: the Creator gives and forgives but humans get and forget".

"Like to think of Nature as an unlimited broadcasting station through which the Creator speaks to us every day if we would only tune in".

"Don't ever let people dull your shine. Be a beacon and glow. Just be you. Don't try to please anyone. Just walk your talk and talk your walk. Be happy in the now, for tomorrow may never come".

"Always start each day knowing that you are loved and needed. That we are still alive for a reason and we are stronger than we think".

About the Author
Kiri Dewes
Poetry

http://kotukudreaming.maori.nz

Story-teller, Composer and Writer of stories, poems, and songs for schools, Culture Clubs in New Zealand, Australia, and The International Society of Poets, America.

Published works in Australia, New Zealand, and the U.S.A.

Cultural Advisor for Arohanui Creative Arts, Melbourne.

International Poet of distinction.

National and International judge for Maori Cultural Competitions.

www.ingramcontent.com/pod-product-compliance
Lightning Source LLC
Chambersburg PA
CBHW070312010526
44107CB00056B/2566